Dr. Dre

by C.F. Earl

Superstars of Hip-Hop

Alicia Keys

Beyoncé

Black Eyed Peas

Ciara

Dr. Dre

Drake

Eminem

50 Cent

Flo Rida

Hip Hop:
A Short History

Jay-Z

Kanye West

Lil Wayne

LL Cool J

Ludacris

Mary J. Blige

Notorious B.I.G.

Rihanna

Sean "Diddy" Combs

Snoop Dogg

T.I.

T-Pain

Timbaland

Tupac

Usher

Dr. Dre

by C.F. Earl

Mason Crest

Dr. Dre

Mason Crest
370 Reed Road
Broomall, Pennsylvania 19008
www.masoncrest.com

Printed and bound in the United States of America.

First printing
9 8 7 6 5 4 3 2 1

Library of Congress Cataloging-in-Publication Data

Earl, C. F.
  Dr. Dre / by C.F. Earl.
      p. cm. – (Superstars of hip hop)
  Includes index.
  ISBN 978-1-4222-2517-2 (hardcover) – ISBN 978-1-4222-2508-0 (series hardcover) – ISBN 978-1-4222-9219-8 (ebook)
  1. Dr. Dre, 1965–-Juvenile literature. 2. Rap musicians–United States–Biography–Juvenile literature. I. Title.
  ML3930.D7E27 2012
  782.421649092–dc22
  [B]
                              2011005428

Produced by Harding House Publishing Services, Inc.
www.hardinghousepages.com
Interior Design by MK Bassett-Harvey.
Cover design by Torque Advertising & Design.

Publisher's notes:
• All quotations in this book come from original sources and contain the spelling and grammatical inconsistencies of the original text.
• The Web sites mentioned in this book were active at the time of publication. The publisher is not responsible for Web sites that have changed their addresses or discontinued operation since the date of publication. The publisher will review and update the Web site addresses each time the book is reprinted.

DISCLAIMER: The following story has been thoroughly researched, and to the best of our knowledge, represents a true story. While every possible effort has been made to ensure accuracy, the publisher will not assume liability for damages caused by inaccuracies in the data, and makes no warranty on the accuracy of the information contained herein. This story has not been authorized nor endorsed by Dr. Dre.

Contents

Hip-Hop lingo

A **turntable** is the part of a phonograph (record player) that holds the plastic record and turns around under the needle. Sometimes a record player is called a turntable, too.

Records are groups of songs played on plastic discs by a phonograph. Today, a lot of people still call CDs and MP3s "records."

R&B stands for "rhythm and blues." It's a kind of music that African Americans made popular in the 1940s. It has a very strong beat. Today, it's a style of music that's a lot like hip-hop.

An **amplifier** is a piece of equipment that makes sound louder.

A **mixer** is a piece of equipment that takes the signals coming from different instruments and microphones and puts them together so they can be recorded.

Rap is a kind of music where rhymes are chanted, often with music in the background. When people rap, they make up these rhymes, sometimes off the top of their heads.

DJ is short for disc jockey. A DJ plays music on the radio or at a party and announces the songs.

A **single** is a song that is sold by itself.

A **record label** is a company that produces music for singers and groups and puts out CDs.

An **album** is a group of songs collected together on a CD.

Chapter 1

The Doc at the Top

Dr. Dre watched Eminem from backstage. Eminem was in his hometown of Detroit. He was performing as part of the 2010 Home and Home Tour with Jay-Z.

Dre had given Eminem the chance to get this far. He'd signed Em when no one would. Now, his risk had paid off. And Dre was about to join his friend onstage in front of thousands and thousands of screaming fans.

The fans knew Dre. They knew his music, too. Dr. Dre had been making huge hip-hop hits for more than twenty years. His life in the rap game started at a very early age. He'd reached places most people never thought he would.

After Dre and Em's performance, Eminem started the crowd chanting "De-tox. De-tox. De-tox." It was the name of an album Dre had been working on for years. But he'd never put it out. The fans wanted more Dr. Dre. He told the crowd: "I'm coming!"

Dre knew how to please his fans. He'd been doing it since he was very young.

Verna Griffin, Dr. Dre's mother, wrote a book in which she described her family's experiences in Compton and her son Andre's early life. *Privileged to Live: A Mother's Story of Survival* was published in 2005.

Early Life

Dr. Dre was born Andre Young. He was born on February 18, 1965 in Compton, California. Compton was a suburb of Los Angeles. It was a tough place to live. Some people turned to using drugs to get away from their troubles. Others became part of gangs.

Andre's mother, Verna, was just sixteen when she had Andre. For a little while, she was married to Andre's father, Theodore. It was a hard relationship, though. Theodore didn't treat Verna well. Soon, Verna left Theodore. She took baby Andre with her. She couldn't raise Andre around Theodore. So, Verna found a job as an office clerk. She was going to raise Andre on her own.

Even when he was just a baby, Verna could see Andre loved music. She could see that listening to music calmed him down when he was upset.

It wasn't long before she saw Andre also loved words. Andre's grandmother liked to recite poems for him. Andre liked to memorize the poems.

By the time Andre was four, he was already using his mother's **turntable**. When Verna had friends over or threw a party, Andre would play **records**. Verna was a fan of **R&B** music. She had records by James Brown, Aretha Franklin, Martha and the Vandellas, and many others. Listening to these records gave Andre an even deeper love of music.

After leaving Theodore, Verna married a man named Curtis Crayon. They had three children together, though two died when they were very young. The relationship didn't work out between Verna and Curtis, though.

Later, Verna married Warren Griffin. He had three daughters and a son, adding more kids to Andre and Verna's family.

Wheels of Steel

As Andre grew older, Verna saw that some of his friends always had money. She thought they might be selling drugs.

Verna had always worried that Andre would be drawn to the money drugs could bring. She told Andre, "Fast money is not good money."

In Compton, Verna knew that her son and his friends could be making money by breaking the law. The city was dangerous. Verna also worried about gangs. The Crips and Bloods, two major gangs, battled for the right to run the streets. Andre told Verna that he'd never join either gang.

As a teenager, Andre enrolled in Centennial High School in Compton. His grades were low, though. School was tough for Andre, because he was always thinking about music.

By the time he was in high school, Andre was making lots of music, too. He had gotten two turntables, an **amplifier**, and a music **mixer**. With these new tools, Andre made beats, songs, and sounds. He called his turntables his "steel wheels."

Andre loved to play his music as loud as he could. Verna always put up with the volume because the loud music was better than the trouble Andre could find in the street. When she came home and heard the music, she knew her kids were at home safe.

Around the same time, **rap** music was becoming very popular. Sometimes, Andre would sneak into Los Angeles at night. There, he could hear the newest hip-hop acts in nightclubs. Andre loved the feeling at the shows he saw.

Soon, he started to **DJ** parties to make extra money. Andre performed using the name Dr. J. Andre took the name because Julius "Dr. J." Erving was his favorite basketball player. After a little while, Andre changed his name to Dr. Dre, a mix of Dr. J and his first name.

Dr. Dre became the DJ at a club called Eve After Dark. He worked there every night. He made fifty dollars each time he performed. While working there, Dre met a young man named Antoine Carraby. Carraby would later become DJ Yella and work with Dre on music.

Dre's music was taking away from his time at school. He'd often skip school to make music. After he graduated from high school, Dre started going to an adult school in Compton. His mother Verna wanted Dre to get a good job with his education. Dre ended up dropping out, though. He wanted to focus on music.

The Birth of N.W.A.

Now that he wasn't going to school, Dre joined a group called World Class Wreckin' Cru. Alonzo Williams had formed the group. He also owned the Eve After Dark club. Antoine Carraby, who Dre met at the club, joined the group too. He started using the name DJ Yella.

World Class Wreckin' Cru made electro-hop music, a special type of hip-hop. Electro-hop was very popular in the early 1980s.

World Class Wreckin' Cru performed some shows in Los Angeles clubs. The group wore shiny clothes and other costumes. They wanted people to have a good time.

In 1985, the group put out a **single** called "Surgery." It became a huge hit in the Los Angeles area. The group sold around 50,000 copies of the song. Dr. Dre's turntables were a huge part of the song.

The next year, Dr. Dre met rapper Ice Cube. The two worked together on music for a local **record label**. The label was called Ruthless Records. A rapper named Eazy-E owned Ruthless.

Eazy-E wanted Ruthless to focus on gangsta rap. Gangsta rap was a new kind of hip-hop. It wasn't about partying, falling in love,

THE **SOURCE**

THE MAGAZINE OF HIP-HOP MUSIC, CULTURE & POLITICS

JUNE 1995 • NO. 6
UK $2.95-UK £2.00-CANADA $3

The influencial rapper Eazy-E is pictured on a magazine cover shortly after his death in 1995. Eazy-E invited Dr. Dre to join the group N.W.A in 1986; together, they helped transform gangsta rap from an underground phenomenon into a mainstream music style.

or having a good time, like most rap at the time. It was about life in tough neighborhoods like Compton.

Eazy-E was forming a new group, and he wanted both Dr. Dre and Ice Cube to join. The new group was called N.W.A. Along with Dre, Ice Cube, and Eazy-E, rappers DJ Yella, MC Ren, and Arabian Prince also joined the group.

The group's first **album** came out in 1987. It was called *N.W.A. and the Posse*. The album had songs like "Panic Zone," "Fat Girl," "Dopeman," and "Tuffest Man Alive."

Many of the songs weren't actually N.W.A. songs. Instead, many were songs Eazy-E had worked on by himself, before he formed N.W.A. That meant the songs weren't as gangsta as N.W.A.'s later songs. "Dopeman" was the first song to feature all the members of N.W.A.

The album sold very well for a new group. Overall, it sold more than 500,000 copies.

But the group wanted to do more than sell records. They wanted to say something with their music. They wanted to tell the true story of life in Compton.

At night, people living in Compton could hear gunfights between gangs. Drug deals went down on the street corners. The police were always around, and it made people feel like they'd done something wrong, even if they didn't do anything. N.W.A. wanted to show people their world, even if it was hard to hear about.

The group started work on their next album. When the album hit stores in 1988, it would change rap forever.

Hip-Hop lingo

Something that is a **classic** is likely to be popular for a long time.

Lyrics are the words in a song.

FBI stands for Federal Bureau of Investigation. The FBI are the police for the whole United States.

The **charts** are lists of the best-selling songs and albums for a week.

A **traitor** is someone who does something to break the trust people have in him.

Chapter 2

Songs for the Neighborhood

N.W.A.'s next album was called *Straight Outta Compton*. The album came out on August 8, 1988. Dr. Dre and DJ Yella worked together to make the beats for the album. Rappers Ice Cube and MC Ren wrote many of the album's **lyrics**. A rapper named the D.O.C. also helped on many of the songs.

Today, many people think that *Straight Outta Compton* is a **classic**. Some think it changed rap more than any other album before it.

When *Straight Outta Compton* came out, though, some people were shocked. They thought that the album was bad music with a bad message. They didn't like the lyrics. They said the songs were full of violence and swearing.

N.W.A. saw it differently. They said the album's lyrics were all about living in Compton. When they rapped about violence or drugs, it was because that's what Compton could be like. They didn't make up the gangsta life, they just rapped about it when no one else did.

One song, though, made people very mad. In the song, N.W.A. raps about the police. They rap about how they felt the police were treating black people badly. Some lines go further, talking about hurting or killing cops. The song was about the anger many people felt about how the police treated them. But a lot of people said it went way too far.

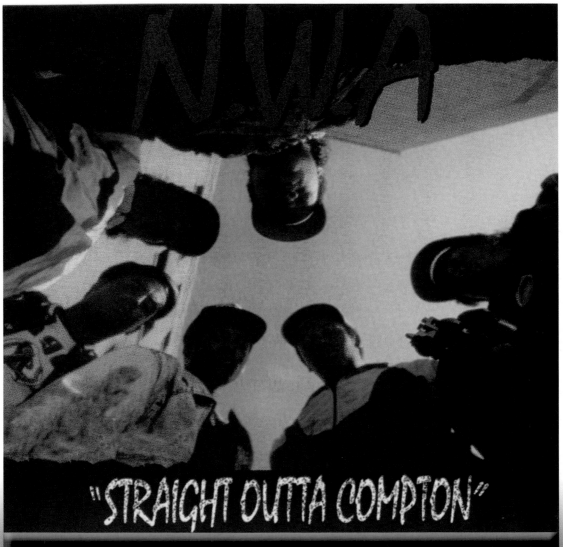

"STRAIGHT OUTTA COMPTON"

The cover of *Straight Outta Compton*, N.W.A's controversial 1988 album. Although radio stations refused to play songs from the album, public outrage over the explicit lyrics fueled a wave of publicity that helped *Straight Outta Compton* sell millions of copies.

N.W.A.'s music didn't get played on TV or the radio because of their lyrics. But it didn't matter. Their songs became hits without the radio. Their song about the police became one of their biggest hits. The song "Straight Outta Compton" also became a huge success.

With help from those songs and others, *Straight Outta Compton* sold very well. In just a few years, it sold more than two million copies. Today, the album has sold more than three million.

But not everyone was a fan. The album's lyrics were still upsetting a lot of people. The **FBI** sent Ruthless Records a letter warning them not to put out music that talked about hurting police. A lawyer named Jack Thompson tried to make it so no one could sell the album. He said the album's lyrics were so bad they were a crime.

But no matter what some people thought, N.W.A. was allowed to keep making the music they wanted to. Even though it was hard for some people to hear.

People wanted to hear N.W.A.'s music because so many people were talking about it. Even if some said it was terrible, people wanted to hear what the fuss was about. The more people talked about the album's lyrics, the more people wanted to hear them.

N.W.A. Without Ice Cube

N.W.A. had become the biggest group in rap. *Straight Outta Compton* was a huge success. But not everyone in the group was happy about the way things were going.

Ice Cube didn't like how the money was being split up. He had worked on most of the lyrics for *Straight Outta Compton*. He thought he should be making more money from the album. In the end, though, he couldn't work out a deal with the group. Ice Cube left N.W.A. in 1989.

Without Ice Cube, the group kept going. They started work on their next album, *100 Miles and Runnin'*. The album was a short one, with just five songs. *100 Miles and Runnin'* was released in 1990. It was the first N.W.A. album made without Ice Cube.

100 Miles and Runnin' was produced by Dr. Dre. The D.O.C. and MC Ren wrote the lyrics.

N.W.A.'s Last Album

It wasn't long before N.W.A. was ready to make their next album. It was called *Efil4zaggin*.

This album was released on May 28, 1991. The week it came out, the album hit number two on the **charts**. The next week, it made it to number one. The album stayed in the top ten for seven weeks.

Now that Ice Cube had left N.W.A., Eazy-E, Dr. Dre, and MC Ren rapped on the album. The album had a few songs that dissed Ice Cube for leaving the group. On one track, the group called Ice Cube "Benedict Arnold." Benedict Arnold was a famous **traitor** from American history. They were saying that Ice Cube had betrayed them when he left. Like *Straight Outta Compton*, Dr. Dre produced *Efil4zaggin* with DJ Yella.

Efil4zaggin had a few singles. None were as big as some of the songs from *Straight Outta Compton*. Singles like "Appetite for Destruction," and "Alwayz Into Somethin" were hits, but not in the same way.

Efil4zaggin was the last studio album from N.W.A. Soon, Dre would leave Ruthless Records. The group would soon split up.

The End of N.W.A.

Dr. Dre didn't just produce albums for N.W.A. He also worked on other albums for Ruthless Records. He worked on solo albums for

Eazy-E and The D.O.C. He worked on albums for other Ruthless Records artists, too.

Dr. Dre helped create the sound for Ruthless Records. And his new sound was taking over hip-hop. Many people thought Dre was the best producer in rap. To them, Dre's G-Funk sound *was* West Coast rap.

Dr. Dre contributed slick production to the successful N.W.A albums *100 Miles and Runnin'* (1990) and *Efil4zaggin* (1991). However, the producer, feeling unappreciated for his work, decided to leave Ruthless Records and form his own label.

But Dre didn't feel like Ruthless Records understood his talents. He thought they didn't appreciate his work enough.

Dre made a lot of money at Ruthless. But he still argued with Eazy-E over money. In an interview with *Rolling Stone* magazine, Dre joked that he had so little money he'd need to move back in with his parents.

In 1990, Marion "Suge" Knight and Dr. Dre agreed to form a new hip-hop label, Death Row Records. Knight had a reputation as a dangerous and ruthless man, and he surrounded himself with thugs and convicts.

In 1990, Dre met Marion "Suge" Knight. Knight had been a pro football player. Then he'd worked as singer Bobby Brown's bodyguard. When he met Dre, Knight was working to get people to come to rap concerts in L.A.

The two men became friends quickly. Soon, Knight learned that Dre wasn't happy at Ruthless. He told Dre he knew what they could do to fix the problem. They could start their own record label.

Dre still had a contract with Ruthless and Eazy-E, though. He couldn't do work for other record labels. So, Suge Knight talked to Eazy-E about Dre getting out of the contract. Somehow, he convinced Eazy-E to let Dre leave the label.

That also meant that Dr. Dre was leaving N.W.A. They had been one of the most successful rap groups of their time. They had changed the game with their hard lyrics. N.W.A. made gangsta rap what it is today. They also gave the West Coast its own hip-hop sound. Now, Dre was moving on. Without him, N.W.A. was over.

Hip-Hop lingo

A **soundtrack** is a collection of all the songs on a movie.

Each year, the National Academy of Recording Arts and Sciences gives out the **Grammy Awards** (short for Gramophone Awards)—or Grammys—to people who have done something really big in the music industry.

A **feud** is a fight between two people or groups that goes on a long time.

Funk is a style of music started in the 1960s. It has a strong beat and is often used as dance music.

Chapter 3

Dr. Dre Goes to Death Row

Suge Knight and Dr. Dre named their new company Death Row Records. Like Ruthless Records, Death Row would put out gangsta rap.

Suge Knight wanted to make Death Row the biggest label in rap. He wanted to make every song a hit. And he knew having Dr. Dre on the label was a good start. He was famous from N.W.A., but he also knew how to produce songs.

At Death Row, Knight took care of the business side of things. Dr. Dre took care of making the music.

Dre was the biggest star on Death Row Records when the company first started. He and Knight knew that his first solo album would be a big hit for Death Row.

The Chronic

Dr. Dre's first solo album was called *The Chronic*. It was released in December 1992.

When it came out, *The Chronic* sold very well. Since its release, it's sold more than three million copies.

The Chronic had a few hit singles. The first was called "Nuthin' but A 'G' Thang." Snoop Dogg raps on the song, along with Dre. When it came out, the song shot way up in the charts.

The second single was called "Let Me Ride." The third was called "Dre Day." These songs featured Snoop Dogg, too.

"Mixing loping beats, smooth and gruff voices from the South Central, giggles, snarls and reggae . . . [*The Chronic's*] sounds are as raw and complex and real as life," commented a *Rolling Stone* reviewer. "The music . . . cannot be refuted or easily forgotten."

Snoop and Dre had met earlier in 1992 through Dre's step-brother Warren G. Warren G had been in a group called 213 with Snoop Dogg. When Dre met Snoop, he knew he'd found a new rap star. The two worked on a song for a movie **soundtrack**. After that, Dre signed Snoop Dogg to Death Row Records.

Together, the two rappers went on to make some of the biggest hits in hip-hop. Their work on *The Chronic* is thought to be some of the best West Coast rap. In fact, many people think *The Chronic* is one of the best rap albums ever made. In 2003, *Rolling Stone* put the album in its list of the best 500 albums of all time.

The Chronic helped create the sound of West Coast rap. It proved Dre was one of the best rappers and producers in hip-hop. It was also the first time many rap fans heard of Snoop Dogg.

After *The Chronic*, Dre's special sound became even more popular. His sound was called G-funk—gangsta **funk**. G-funk was a mix of gangsta rap beats and the funk Dr. Dre grew up with. It had a low, bass-heavy sound. G-funk was a big part of what made West Coast rap different from other kinds of rap music.

In 1993, Dr. Dre won a **Grammy Award** for the song "Let Me Ride." The award was for Best Rap Solo Performance. It was Dre's first Grammy. But it wasn't his last.

Snoop Dogg

After *The Chronic* came out in 1992, Snoop Dogg was a star. The new rapper's flow was different from other rappers. He was laid back. He was cool. And he was a great rapper.

When Dre met Snoop, he knew Snoop had a lot of talent. When Dre signed Snoop to Death Row, the two started work on Snoop's first album.

The album was called *Doggystyle*. It came out on November 23, 1993. Dr. Dre produced every song on the album.

The first single from *Doggystyle* was called "Who Am I (What's My Name)?" The single was popular, but the second single is still a hip-hop classic today. It was called "Gin and Juice." That song made Snoop even more famous.

Doggystyle was a huge success. It has sold more than four million albums. *Doggystyle* helped make Dr. Dre even more famous, too. His production and his sound helped make the album a hit.

Death Row artists Tupac Shakur (left) and Snoop Dogg (center) pose with label cofounder Suge Knight for a promotional photo. *The Chronic* helped make Snoop Dogg into a major rap star. Dr. Dre produced Snoop's first solo album, *Doggystyle* (1993).

Trouble at Death Row

By 1995, Dre didn't like what Death Row had become. The label was focusing on the battle between East Coast and West Coast rap. Suge Knight encouraged the battle. But Dre didn't want to have anything to do with it. He just wanted to make music.

Dre was also getting tired of Suge Knight. He was starting to think Knight was out of control. Knight wasn't handling money well. Dre was worried Knight was going to hurt someone, too.

Knight had been giving jobs at Death Row to his friends. Mostly, that meant members of Knight's gang worked at the label.

Dre ended up leaving Death Row in 1995. It was a nasty split for Dre and the label. Suge Knight wouldn't let Dre take any of the music he'd worked on there. Rappers at Death Row started calling Dre a traitor.

But Dre left the label at just the right time. He knew the East Coast-against-the-West Coast **feud** couldn't end well. He was right. In September 1996, rapper Tupac was killed in Los Angeles. In 1997, Notorious B.I.G. was killed as well. Tupac had been signed to Death Row. He'd even worked with Dre on a song called "California Love."

Many people thought the rap war between the coasts led to Tupac and Biggie's deaths. Some think that Suge Knight had something to do with both killings.

No matter what, Dre was done with Death Row. He was ready to move on. And he wanted to be in charge of his own life.

Hip-Hop lingo

A **compilation** is a collection of different kinds of songs that have been put together on one album.

Critics are people who judge artistic works and say what is good and what is bad about them.

Demos are rough recordings to give an idea of what an artist can do.

A **mixtape** is a collection of a few songs put on a CD or given away for free on the Internet without being professionally recorded.

Chapter 4

Aftermath

After leaving Death Row, Dre made some big changes to his life. First, he married his long-time girlfriend Nicole. He stopped going to parties and staying up all night. Instead, Dre started coming home to his wife and their two kids.

Dre also started his own label. He called the company Aftermath Entertainment. Dre started making new music right away.

His first project was called *Dr. Dre Presents the Aftermath*. The album was a **compilation**. It had songs from different artists and producers together on the same album. It was a way for Dre to show off the talent on his new label.

The Aftermath sold well enough when it came out in 1996. But **critics** said the producers who made beats for the album weren't as talented as Dre. They said the album needed more beats from Dre.

In 1997, Aftermath Entertainment put out another compilation album. It was called *The Firm: The Album*. Like *The Aftermath*, *The Firm* sold well. But, again, something was missing. That something was Dr. Dre. Soon, though, he'd be back in a major way.

Eminem

In 1998, Dr. Dre visited his friend Jimmy Iovine. Iovine worked for Interscope Records. Dre and Iovine often listened to **demos** of new artists together. Iovine told Dre he wanted his opinion of a new demo. It was from a white rapper from Detroit. The rapper's name was Eminem.

Dre liked Eminem's flow. He thought the younger rapper had real talent. Later, Dre told VH1 that he knew he had to work with Eminem as soon as he heard the demo.

Eminem and Dr. Dre perform together at a 2000 concert in Seattle. When Eminem's first two albums were criticized for lyrics that seemed to advocate violence toward women and gays, Dre supported the controversial rapper.

In 1998, Dr. Dre was impressed when he heard a demo tape by an unknown white rapper who performed under the name Eminem. Dre signed Eminem to his Aftermath Entertainment label, and produced his first two albums.

Dre knew signing a white rapper could be a big risk. Some people didn't think a white rapper could succeed. They thought hip-hop fans wouldn't listen to a white rapper. Many white rappers before Eminem had been silly. No one had taken them seriously.

But Dre saw things differently. He knew Eminem could be popular with both black and white hip-hop fans. He understood that hip-hop could speak to many people, no matter their race.

Dre also saw that hip-hop wasn't just a voice for young black people. It was becoming a voice for all young people. It was becoming something all people could enjoy.

Dre signed Eminem to his label. He and Eminem went to work on Em's first album. It was called *The Slim Shady LP*. Dre produced a few beats for the album. He made the beat for the first single from the album. The single was called "My Name Is." Dre also rapped on Eminem's song "Guilty Conscience."

The album made Eminem a star. It also proved Dre was still one of the best producers in hip-hop.

2001

After his work on *The Slim Shady*, Dre's fans wanted to hear more from him. And he was ready to give the people what they wanted.

In 1999, Dre put out his first album since *The Chronic*. This one was called *2001*.

When *2001* came out on November 16, it was a huge success. In its first week, the album sold 516,000 copies. It reached number two on the album charts, too.

2001 had three singles. The first was called "Still D.R.E." Like the most popular songs from *The Chronic*, "Still D.R.E." featured Snoop Dogg.

The next single featured Eminem. The song was called "Forgot About Dre." The song and its music video were a hit. So was the

SPECIAL FIRST ANNIVERSARY ISSUE

BLAZE

EXCLUSIVE! DISSECTING THE '90s WITH

DR. DRE & SNOOP

Dr. Dre and Snoop Dogg are featured on the cover of *Blaze* magazine. The two rappers teamed up again on Dre's highly successful follow-up to *The Chronic*, *Dr. Dre 2001*. The album was praised by critics and sold more than 6 million copies.

next single, "The Next Episode." That song featured Snoop Dogg, too.

2001 has sold more than seven million copies in the United States. It sold more than *The Chronic. 2001* is Dre's best-selling album. Fans and critics loved the album. It even won Dre and Eminem a Grammy for "Forgot About Dre."

Eminem (left) and Dre (right) discovered the unknown rapper 50 Cent and agreed to jointly produce his first album. 50 Cent's debut, *Get Rich or Die Tryin'*, was a smash success that reached number one on *Billboard* magazine's album chart.

2001 proved that Dre was still one of the best artists in rap. His production sound was still popular. His rhymes still spoke to people. Even seven years after *The Chronic*, Dre still had it.

50 Cent

In 2002, Eminem heard a **mixtape** from a New York rapper named 50 Cent. Em liked the songs on the mixtape a lot. He asked 50 to fly to L.A. to meet Dr. Dre.

Dre and Em signed 50 Cent after the meeting. 50 would be part of Aftermath and Shady Records, Eminem's new label.

50 Cent's first album was called *Get Rich or Die Tryin'*. Dre produced the first single from the album. It was called "In da Club." When it came out, the song was everywhere. It was on the radio. The music video was on TV. The song blasted on car stereos. People danced to it at clubs across the country.

With "In da Club," Dre made sure that 50's new album would be a hit. When the album came out, it sold almost 900,000 copies in one week. It was the number-one album in the country for six weeks. In three weeks, the album had sold more than two million copies.

Dre signed Eminem when no one would. Now, he'd given 50 Cent a chance. Dre's chances were paying off for him. Just like in the 1990s, Dre was helping to shape hip-hop.

Hip-Hop lingo

A song is **leaked** if people start listening to it before it is officially released.

Chapter 5

Here to Stay

Dre was on top of the music world. He'd changed the rap game forever while he was with N.W.A. *The Chronic* and *2001* had both become hip-hop classics. He'd also brought the rap world two of its biggest artists—Eminem and 50 Cent.

In 2008, Dre moved into another part of the music business. He started a brand of headphones called Beats by Dr. Dre. He wanted to make the best headphones around. Lady Gaga and Diddy have both made special headphones for Beats.

In 2009, Beats worked with computer company HP. HP sold a pair of Beats headphones with some of their computers. Dre was also in a Dr. Pepper commercial. The commercial helped spread the word about Beats.

The Dr. Pepper commercial was important for another reason, too. The music in the ad was taken from Dr. Dre's album *Detox*. Dre has been working on *Detox* since 2003. The album has never been released, though.

Detox

To Dr. Dre fans, *Detox* is already well known. It's famous, even though nobody has ever listened to it. *Detox* will be Dr. Dre's first album since 2001.

Dre has been working on *Detox* for years. A few times, Dre told people the album was going to come out. But it was never released.

Dr. Dre started working on *Detox* in 2003. The album was meant to come out in 2005. Then, Dre stopped working on *Detox* to help with other artists from Aftermath. The release for *Detox* was pushed back. Dre didn't set a new release date, though.

Over the next few years, Dr. Dre kept talking about *Detox*. In 2007, Dre told a radio station that he'd made a bunch of songs for the album. At the MTV Video Music Awards that year, he told fans his album was on its way. 50 Cent told an interviewer he'd worked on songs for *Detox*, too.

In 2008, Dre told his fans *Detox* would come out after Eminem's *Relapse*. Snoop Dogg also told an interviewer that Dre had finished many songs for the album. Eminem's album came out in 2009. But *Detox* still didn't appear.

The first official music from *Detox* came out in 2009. It was part of the Dr. Pepper commercial.

No one is sure how many songs Dre has made for *Detox*. His fans don't know which artists will be featured on the album either. Jay-Z, Eminem, and 50 Cent are rumored to have worked on *Detox*. Many others have been linked with the album, too. Ice Cube, Raekwon, and The Game have all been mentioned. Lady Gaga, Busta Rhymes, and Mary J. Blige have been talked about, too. People watched Dre's studio, to see who went in. Artists like T.I. and Lil Kim visited sometimes. People wondered if they could be working on *Detox*.

In June 2010, an unfinished song from *Detox* **leaked** online. The song was called "Under Pressure." It was meant to be the first single from *Detox*. "Under Pressure" had no chorus, though. Dre told fans the song wasn't finished. He was mad it had leaked. Dre took the song off *Detox* because of the leak.

In November 2010, a song called "Kush" leaked onto the Internet. People said "Kush" was from *Detox*. "Kush" featured Snoop Dogg and Akon.

Today, Dre is concentrating on singing and developing new talent for Aftermath Entertainment. One of the stars Dre helped to bring into the music business is rapper The Game, whose debut album *The Documentary* (2005) sold more than a million copies.

Not long after the song leaked, it was released online. "Kush" was the first single from *Detox*. Dre saw that people liked it. So he released it as a real single.

In 2011, Dre put out a song called "I Need a Doctor" with Eminem and singer Skylar Grey. Shortly after the song came out, Dre, Em, and Grey performed the song live at the Grammy Awards. In the emotional song, Eminem begs Dr. Dre to return to rap. He also raps about Dre losing his son in 2008 and how hard it has been for the rap legend to finish *Detox*.

"Although I'm from the West Coast, I try to make music that will have a universal appeal," Dre wrote on his website in 2001. "It's always been my desire to make music for the world."

Fans had been waiting for *Detox* for years. Now, "Kush" and "I Need a Doctor" gave them the first taste of the album. Fans started to hope the album might be coming soon. Dre hasn't said just when *Detox* will come out. Some people believe the album will never come out. But whenever it does, his fans are ready.

Looking to the Future

It's hard to say enough about what Dr. Dre has done for rap. With N.W.A., he helped change the message and sound of hip-hop. Dre and the group made rap even more popular with *Straight Outta Compton*.

Dre helped start Death Row Records, too. Now, it's one of the biggest labels in rap history. He's helped many artists become stars. He helped bring Snoop Dogg, Eminem, and 50 Cent to the world. For years, Dr. Dre has shaped hip-hop. Today, he's still doing it.

Fans are waiting for Dre to release *Detox*. Dre is hard at work on lots of different things, though. He's producing albums, making sure the sound is just right. Dre's also running Aftermath Entertainment and Beats by Dre. He's working with new artists like Kendrick Lamar, too.

Dre has done lots of things. He always has new ideas to work on. Whatever he does, his fans will be ready. They're always hungry for whatever Dre has to offer.

1965	Andre Young is born in Compton, California, on February 18.
1986	Dr. Dre joins four other rappers to form the hip-hop group N.W.A.
1989	N.W.A.'s second album, *Straight Outta Compton*, soars to the top of the hip-hop charts and causes a national outrage for advocating violence against the police.
1991	*Efil4zaggin* is released by N.W.A. Dre quits N.W.A. and founds Death Row Records with Marion "Suge" Knight. Dre is charged with assaulting a TV host in a nightclub; he is sentenced to house arrest.
1992	Dre is charged with assaulting a New Orleans police officer and is again placed on house arrest; *The Chronic*, Dre's first album for Death Row Records, is released. Dre punches a record producer and is sentenced to house arrest.
1994	Dre is arrested for drunken driving and, because he violated his probation on the 1992 assault charge, is sentenced to five months in prison, which he begins serving in 1995.
1995	The East Coast-West Coast feud heats up when Knight insults rival record producer Sean "Puffy" Combs at the *Source* magazine awards show. After his release from prison, Dre vows to stay out of trouble with the law. He leaves Death Row and starts his own label, Aftermath Entertainment.
1996	Death Row rapper Tupac is murdered in a drive-by shooting in September.
1997	Notorious B.I.G., who records for Combs's Bad Boy Entertainment label, is murdered in a drive-by shooting in March.

1998   After hearing a demo tape made by Eminem, Dre signs the young rapper to a record contract.

1999   Dre releases *Dr. Dre 2001*, which receives good reviews because it reflects Dre's return to his gangsta roots.

2001   *The Marshall Mathers LP*, produced by Dre, is nominated for a Grammy Award as Album of the Year; Dre acts in two films, *The Wash* and *Training Day*; donated $1 million to aid the victims of the September 11 terrorist attacks.

Dr. Dre sells part of his share of Aftermath Entertainment to Interscope Records and earns about $52 million as a result.

2002   Dre and Eminem sign rapper 50 Cent to a record contract and produce his first album, *Get Rich or Die Tryin'*.

2004   Dre is assaulted by a fan at the *Vibe* Awards, where he is presented the magazine's Legend Award; later, it is alleged the assailant was paid by Suge Knight to punch Dre. Knight denies the charge.

2005   Dre produces *The Documentary*, the debut album for rapper The Game that soars to the top of the hip-hop charts. Dre donates $1 million to aid the victims of Hurricane Katrina.

2008   Dr. Dre releases his high-performance brand of headphone in July, called Beats by Dr. Dre.

Dre's son Andre, Jr. dies at 20.

2009   Dr. Pepper hires Dre to be the face of its soda; he gives his fans a snippet of *Detox* in the commercials.

2011   Dr. Dre releases "I Need a Doctor" featuring Eminem and Skylar Grey. The song is a single from the unreleased *Detox*.

In Books

Baker, Soren. *The History of Rap and Hip Hop*. San Diego, Calif.: Lucent, 2006.

Comissiong, Solomon W. F. *How Jamal Discovered Hip-Hop Culture*. New York: Xlibris, 2008.

Cornish, Melanie. *The History of Hip Hop*. New York: Crabtree, 2009.

Czekaj, Jef. *Hip and Hop, Don't Stop!* New York: Hyperion, 2010.

Haskins, Jim. *One Nation Under a Groove: Rap Music and Its Roots*. New York: Jump at the Sun, 2000.

Hatch, Thomas. *A History of Hip-Hop: The Roots of Rap*. Portsmouth, N.H.: Red Bricklearning, 2005.

Websites

Aftermath Entertainment
www.aftermath-entertainment.com

Dr. Dre's Discovery of Eminem
www.vh1.com/artists/interview/1455173/06132002/dr_dre.jhtml

Dr. Dre's Official Website
www.beatsbydre.com

Dre on MTV
www.mtv.com/music/artist/dr_dre/artist.jhtml

Discography
Albums with N.W.A.

1987   N.W.A. and the Posse

1988   Stralght Outta Compton

1990   100 Miles and Runnin'

1991   Efil4zaggin

Solo Albums

1992   The Chronic

1996   Dr. Dre Presents. . . The Aftermath

1999   2001

2002   Chronicle: Best of the Work

Index

About the Author

C.F. Earl is a writer living and working in Binghamton, New York. Earl writes mostly on social and historical topics, including health, the military, and finances. An avid student of the world around him, and particularly fascinated with almost any current issue, C.F. Earl hopes to continue to write for books, websites, and other publications for as long as he is able.

Picture Credits